History of the
Fur Trade

by Leo Frank

 HOUGHTON MIFFLIN HARCOURT
School Publishers

PHOTOGRAPHY CREDITS: Cover © INTERFOTO Pressebildagentur/Alamy. Title page © Tania Thomson/Shutterstock. 2 Photodisc/Getty Images. 3 Comstock/Jupiterimages. 4 © Tania Thomson/Shutterstock. 5 (l) (r) The Granger Collection, New York. 8 Photodisc/Getty Images. 10 MPI/Hulton Archive/Getty Images. 11 © North Wind Picture Archives/Alamy. 12 © INTERFOTO Pressebildagentur/Alamy. 13 Private Collection, Peter Newark American Pictures/The Bridgeman Art Library. 14 © Bettmann/CORBIS. 17 The Art Archive/Gift of Ruth Koerner Oliver/Buffalo Bill Historical Center, Cody, Wyoming/6921.1.

Printed in China

ISBN-10: 0-544-04793-1
ISBN-13: 978-0-544-04793-8

11 12 13 14 0940 19 18 17 16
4500569761

Table of Contents

The Trap Is Set

It is the middle of April. The sun shines brightly on the snow-covered wilderness. A lone trapper moves deliberately through a wooded area. He searches for signs of beavers.

After an hour, the trapper spots a group of willow tree stumps with telltale teeth marks. Nearby he locates a stream. On one side, he finds a dam of branches, twigs, and mud that has created a large pond. Beavers!

The trapper enters the pond. It is like stepping into liquid ice. Though his feet cramp instantly, he must stay in the freezing water, which hides his human scent. In this way, he can set his traps without the beavers being aware of his presence.

The trapper carefully opens the jaws of a metal trap. He secures it in place with a metal spike and chain. He baits the trap with a willow twig dipped in beaver musk. The trap is designed to snap shut on a beaver's paw and hold the beaver under water until it drowns. But if the beaver manages to escape somehow, the trapper will try again.

Trapping beavers was grisly, difficult work. It may sound terribly cruel to us today. But in the early nineteenth century, hundreds of American trappers scoured the continent for just that purpose. The trappers traveled into rugged valleys, over towering mountain ranges, and across great rivers where few white men had been before. Out in the unforgiving wilderness, many trappers were hurt. Some trappers lost their lives. Many, many beavers were killed.

Without knowing it, the trappers forever changed the landscape and ecology of the western United States. These trappers and the beavers they killed are an important part of the story of how the West was settled.

The search for the beaver (*Castor canadensis*) resulted in the exploration of large parts of the western United States.

The Hat That Made History

Why were hunters trapping beavers? For food? To stop the damming of rivers and their tributaries? In fact, people wanted beaver pelts to make fashionable hats.

From the seventeenth century through the beginning of the nineteenth century, beaver pelts were in great demand in Europe. The soft fur was used to make various pieces of clothing, but hats were the most popular. Fur hats kept people warm and dry. Perhaps more significantly, the hats distinguished the rich from the poor. Only wealthy people could afford to own a hat made from beaver fur.

More Than a Head Warmer

From the mid-1600s to the 1830s, hats made of beaver fur dominated men's hat styles.

Early Fur Trade

Catching and trading animal furs was a profitable business as early as the 1500s. North American Indians traded beaver pelts to European explorers for manufactured objects they did not have, such as firearms, brass kettles, metal knives, and fishhooks.

Over time, different groups became involved in the fur trade, including the first European settlers in North America. Through the 1600s and 1700s, in what is now Canada, British and French fur traders competed to dominate the trade. Sometimes, they fought each other.

The European fur traders also fought with North American Indians. Both the Indians and the European fur traders wanted control of the rivers and land where the beavers lived. Both understood the value of the beaver fur. In those days, beaver pelts were like cash. The pelts could buy anything.

Before Traps Before the invention of metal traps, North American Indians used other methods to catch beavers. One way was to break down a beaver dam and spear the animals as they tried to escape. Another was to cut a hole in the ice over a pond and catch the beavers when they surfaced for air.

North America, 1804

Louisiana
Purchase

UNITED
STATES

The Lewis and Clark
Expedition ——

Mississippi
River

The Lewis and Clark **Expedition** explored land
west of the Mississippi River.

Lewis and Clark

Beavers were hunted aggressively in the eastern United
States and Canada through the early 1800s. By that time,
the beaver population in this range was in serious decline.
Despite this, the high demand for beaver fur continued.
People still wanted beaver hats and were willing to pay a
premium to get them. The United States government and
fur traders knew this was a rich opportunity. More beaver
pelts meant more work and more trade—a healthier
economy.

Then in 1804, events occurred that would change the
beaver fur trade forever. That year, President Thomas
Jefferson sent his personal secretary Captain Meriwether
Lewis and Lieutenant William Clark on an important trek
to the West.

A year earlier, the United States had roughly doubled in size as a result of the Louisiana Purchase. A large part of the newly acquired 828,000 square miles was unexplored. President Jefferson sent Lewis and Clark to survey part of the land.

Before their departure, the President had many questions about the land. Did the mountain ranges present difficult barriers for westward travelers? Were the rivers suitable for transporting people and goods? Were the Native Americans friendly?

President Jefferson and the fur traders were hopeful about the prospect of finding beavers in the uncharted land. Lewis and Clark were supposed to map out where the beavers were. They were also supposed to explore trade routes and to develop friendly relations with Native Americans.

There was much anticipation and excitement when Lewis and Clark returned from their adventure in 1806. The explorers brought back a wealth of information. And for the fur traders, they fulfilled their hopes. Beavers, they reported, were everywhere.

Fur, Inc.

At the beginning of the 1800s, much of the fur trade in the United States was handled by two large companies. These companies paid trappers to catch beavers. They then sold the pelts in Europe. After the Lewis and Clark Expedition, the companies hired more trappers. They gave the trappers the lofty goal of catching all the beavers that could be found.

One of the companies, the Hudson's Bay Company, was among the first large corporations in North America. For about one hundred years, the company collected and sold approximately 50,000 beaver pelts each year!

German immigrant John Jacob Astor founded the other company, the American Fur Company, in 1809. Astor had first learned about the fur trade as a young man while traveling to the United States. In addition to his company, Astor established a fur-trading base called Astoria at the mouth of the Columbia River in what is now Oregon. Trappers would sell furs at the base. Then the pelts would begin the long journey to Europe. When Astor died, he was the richest man in America. His wealth was traceable directly to the fur trade.

Mountain Men

Who were these trappers who searched the wilderness for beavers? They were called "mountain men." Most were young, adventurous men looking for a way to earn good money. Many were skilled hunters who knew how to track, or follow, and trap and survive in challenging conditions. A few became legends of their time.

What About the Mountain Women? It was not easy for women to share the trapper's life. Some trappers married Native American women. These women were known for having skills that white American women typically did not have. Some wives would help their husbands with their work. But most mountain men chose to go trapping alone or only in the company of other men.

This painting depicts the marriage of a Native American woman to a white trapper.

A Dangerous Life

Mountain men took many risks. Life in the wilderness was full of dangers. The trappers faced attacks from bears, mountain lions, and human enemies. They risked infections from untreated wounds, bites from poisonous animals and insects, and accidental falls. In handmade canoes, they navigated rough rivers and cascading waterfalls. They sometimes faced extreme weather. The mountain men were also at risk for various fatal diseases, such as smallpox, tetanus, and dysentery.

Some trappers carried their furs through snowy terrain.

When the mountain men left civilization for the wilderness, they brought only essential provisions. They carried staples such as sugar, flour, coffee, tea, and salt. They mostly lived off what edible meat they could catch or hunt, from trout to rabbit to deer. If they could not find food, they faced starvation. In some drier parts of the wilderness, water could be difficult to find. So the mountain men had to be wary of dehydration as well.

The mountain men often brought horses to carry their heavy packs. However, if a horse was injured or died, the men were forced to shoulder the packs, which were weighed down by their metal traps.

Yet another challenge was the lack of detailed, reliable maps. The mountain men often had to find their own way through difficult terrain. Becoming lost was always a risk.

A trapper and his heavily laden horse

Learning to Survive To survive, many mountain men copied the techniques of the Native Americans. They wore shoes made from animal skins. They slept in structures made from animal hides. They learned how to track animals using native techniques. The Native Americans taught them how to build canoes.

Some mountain men developed friendships with the Native Americans. But others did not. Sometimes, violent disputes broke out between the Native Americans and the trappers.

James Beckwourth

(1798–c.1866) had a father who was a white plantation owner. His mother was an enslaved black worker. Beckwourth was raised as a free man. In 1824, Beckwourth became a beaver trapper. Later he befriended people of the Crow Nation, who eventually made him a chief. In his years with the Crow, Beckwourth trapped on their land and fought by their side.

The first Rendezvous was held during the summer of 1825 at Henry's Fort on the Green River.

Taking a Summer Break Returning to city life was difficult for some mountain men. Many became accustomed to living without rules. They liked traveling alone or in small groups, sometimes not seeing other human beings for months. They liked sleeping under the stars and surviving off the land.

General William Ashley, a partner in the Rocky Mountain Fur Company, knew that the trappers loved their way of life. He also knew that summertime was when many trappers left the wilderness and traveled east to trade their pelts.

In the spring of 1825, Ashley told several groups of his trappers to gather at a spot along the Green River in Wyoming. There, he planned to cache some supplies. He would also bring materials to trade with Native Americans. Everyone met in early summer and created an event called "the Rendezvous" that would continue every summer for about 15 years. The event's name came from the French word *rendez-vous*, which means "meeting."

At the Rendezvous, trappers traded their beaver pelts, stocked up on supplies, and collected mail—without ever having to leave the wilderness. But the Rendezvous was more than just a place to do business. It was a huge party. There were singing, dancing, and gambling. There were contests. The mountain men sat together and shared stories about their adventures. They were famous for bragging and telling tall tales about what they had done.

True or False? James Bridger was a mountain man known for his outrageous tales that seemed too crazy to be true. But some of them actually happened. Here are two stories Bridger told:

- He said that he could remember when Pikes Peak, a large mountain in Colorado, was just a hole in the ground.

- He said he had an arrow in his back for three years.

Which is true? The second story. Bridger *did* have an arrow in his back until a surgeon at a Rendezvous removed it!

Empty Traps

In the mid-1830s, there was a rumor at a Rendezvous that a sophisticated European had lost his fancy beaver hat while traveling in China. He was unable to replace the hat immediately. So he had a similar hat made from silk. When he returned to Europe, people loved his silk hat. They wanted silk hats, too.

This story may or may not be true. But it is true that beaver hats went out of fashion around that time. People became more interested in silk hats. Also, trappers had been catching and killing beavers for over three decades in the western United States. There weren't many beavers left. By the 1840s, the beaver fur trade was coming to an end.

Opening the West

The work of the beaver trappers was over. Some mountain men resumed their lives in the cities. Some started their own farms. The life of the mountain men was a thing of the past, but what they had seen and done was shaping America's future.

Settlers used the trails of fur trappers to travel west.

People in the eastern United States heard the mountain men's stories and learned about the West. They heard there was fertile land. The stories made them want to head west.

As the mountain men trapped beavers, they created trails. James Beckwourth discovered a mountain pass over the Sierra Nevada range. It is now called Beckwourth Pass.

Another mountain man, Jedediah Strong Smith, rediscovered Wyoming's South Pass, an important pass on the Oregon Trail. Settlers traveled those trails west to start new lives.

Important Events in the History of the American Fur Trade

1500s	Native Americans trade furs with Europeans.
1620	Pilgrims establish Plymouth Colony and begin trading furs.
1670	Hudson's Bay Fur Company is founded.
1803	Louisiana Purchase is signed.
1804–1806	Lewis and Clark Expedition takes place.
1808	John Jacob Astor founds American Fur Company.
1811	Fur trading base of Astoria is established.
1825	First annual Rendezvous is held at Henry's Fort in Wyoming.
1856	With the help of a journalist, mountain man James Beckwourth publishes the popular *The Life and Adventures of James P. Beckwourth, Mountaineer, Scout, Pioneer and Chief of the Crow Nation of Indians.*

Responding

✔ **TARGET SKILL** **Main Ideas and Details** Reread page 4 and identify the main idea of the first paragraph. Which details support this main idea? Copy and complete the web below.

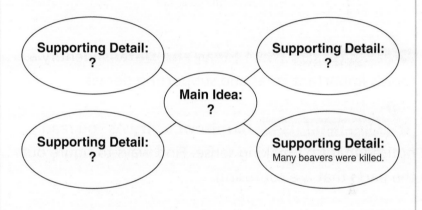

Supporting Detail: ?

Supporting Detail: ?

Main Idea: ?

Supporting Detail: ?

Supporting Detail: Many beavers were killed.

✏ Write About It

Text to World Think about the people, events, and things you read about in *History of the Fur Trade*. Choose one topic that interests you. Then write an outline for a research paper that you might write about that topic.

✔ **TARGET SKILL** **Main Ideas and Details** Identify a topic's important ideas and supporting details.

✔ **TARGET STRATEGY** **Monitor/Clarify** As you read, notice what isn't making sense. Find ways to figure out the parts that are confusing.

GENRE Narrative Nonfiction gives factual information by telling a true story.